# INTERWOVEN
## Uncovering Buried Memories

Linnea Quyen

Presentation by *BookLeaf Publishing*

Web: www.bookleafpub.com

E-mail: info@bookleafpub.com

ISBN: 9789363319882

First edition 2024

*To the first Sarah who became my best friend and never ceased to see the light in me, even when I was enveloped in a deep dark. And to every Sarah I have encountered thereafter. Each of you have been like a guardian angel to me, wherever I have happened to meet you. Thank you 🙏 What a blessing you are.*


*"Your bravery shines brighter than your worries. Always has, and always will." - S* ❤


*To my parents. Without them and every single act done out of sheer will, sacrifice and survival - I would not be here.*


*And to God. Thank You for keeping my parents alive when they had the lowest chance to be. 🙏 Thank You for their lives, that my siblings and I could have ours.*

# PREFACE

This book covers a broad spectrum of memories, from my parents' past to emotional awareness to what is current in my life, to show the interconnectedness of our lives and how God has always been at work, in the center of it all; bringing light into darkness.

# Before

It was fifth grade. My classmates and I were going on a multi-day camping trip – some of our first experiences away from home, sleeping in an unfamiliar bed. However, it was a lot of fun. We were immersed in a variety of activities I hadn't been exposed to but allowed for creativity and independent exploration, such as orienteering/treasure map hunting. I became an immediate fan. It helped that the camp counselors were all friendly and welcoming/inclusive, too.

I began to feel a sense of belonging. A sense of home away from home. It was comforting. By the end of the trip, I wasn't exactly ready to leave.

After having done our share of packing up and helping where we could, my classmates (several who I had become closer friends with) and I were waiting for the rest of the camp to be packed up and buses to be as well, before taking us back to school. Most of these classmates were gathered near me in little groups, talking to each other. I just kind of stood amidst them, feeling

blent in though by myself, scanning; seeing if I
could lend a hand anywhere. When there wasn't
any to be seen, I decided to just sit down right
where I was. Content with myself and who I
was. No thought to anything external. I had a
knack then of being able to muffle out sound and
find a stillness within as well as surrounding me,
no matter what was going on. An inner peace
you might say. .. A camp counselor walked by
and held out a hand for a high-five which I gave.
..

I didn't realize it then, but I belonged without
having to work for it. By just being who I was. ..

As the buses departed, I looked back a last time,
wondering if I would ever be back…

# Reinforced to Abandon Ourselves/Our Collective Pain

I remember always feeling like this compulsion I had in my younger teen years - to look back a little longer at individuals after having passed them to seek connection, to see if they were looking back, just to say a last "bye" - was abnormal. Different. It made me doubt myself. And this was even before the degrading high school labeling... "But what was so wrong about doing that?" the thought always lingered inside my head. This after being ushered on by my mom every time.

...

It hurts there is such a way of parenting that claims to be loving while seeking to be forceful and using authoritative power when the child appears (according to the parent/adult/caretaker) "out of control," "crying for no reason," "faking it," "disrespectful," "rude."

As the wisdom from several responsive parenting resources, including Instagram accounts @maggiewithperspectacles, @drbeckyatgoodinside, @attachmentnerd, and @responsive_parenting, so deftly put it, the child is more than likely acting out of a dysregulated nervous system. They do not know what to do with the overwhelming feelings surging inside their bodies as their adult caretaker tells them that the way they are being isn't the way they are supposed to act. They are not being disrespectful. They do not need disciplining. They are not capable of "obeying" at this point.

~ They are dysregulated = innately good kids with difficult feelings their bodies and minds do not know how to handle yet. ~

But as adults deep in this cycle, do we know how to healthily be with these big feelings? Or have we continually been made to feel that they are not meant to have, undeserving of our attention and understanding – too much. Internalizing it as we are being too much; unable to be handled and cared for when we have and show these big feelings. That it is not safe to be ourselves during those moments. So we hide and suppress. And thus, we have continued to have the same relationship with these big emotions into adulthood.

We have been reinforced to endure our own pain and suffering, as young as infancy. The cry-it-out method. To diminish our own selves. To be approved and liked, even by our own parents...?!

All this internalized pain... where do you think it goes when it has nowhere to be communicated, thus released?

Into the world as collective, deeply-felt pain, hurt, anger, depression, anxiety, loneliness, disease, turmoil – suffering. Retained in the depths of the body and mind in the same forms.

Because we have not learned how to be with our own self, in all of our entirety. Lovingly. Peacefully. Tenderly.

It sits inside of each of us until we are ready to face, hold and look at it with the utmost compassion and love, the way it has been waiting, longing to be. – And deserves to be. It is a part of you. A part of each of us. Every part of ourselves deserves to be seen.

.

"Take no part in the unfruitful works of darkness, but instead expose them. Everything exposed by the light becomes visible, for everything that becomes visible is Light."
(Ephesians 5:11, 13-14)

# Tapped into the Amygdala

There is something significant to how our human brains are able to react and respond to anything. Instinctively, we are made to use the prefrontal cortex (located just behind the forehead, at the forefront of the brain) to make decisions openly, adapt/adjust and problem solve, considering and weighing all the options, to thrive – best serving all individuals involved ideally. But this is without constraints of any kind or external influence.

As we experience incidents that make us doubt ourselves and our decisions, make us feel we are to blame, silence our voices, invoke fear or is abusive in any way, our self-belief is shaken. The confidence and ability to listen to our gut feeling is lowered immensely. We have now turned towards external voices to influence our own approval, self-beliefs, self-talk and decision making.

That fear that lives and grows inside of us – every time it gets triggered by any or a combination of the aforementioned in the previous paragraph, taps into our amygdala (two amygdalae are located in the temporal lobes of the brain, just above the ears [WebMD]). Rather than making decisions set for thriving like the prefrontal cortex, the amygdala reacts in ways that are meant only for survival. Immediate protection. To run, hide, freeze, fight, etc. The more that fear/doubt gets triggered, the more the amygdala gets tapped into, until the brain believes this is how it is supposed to operate – reactively out of the amygdala instead of responsively out of the prefrontal cortex.

This is how we lose trust in our selves. The fear rewires our brain into believing we are as small, pitiful and unworthy as we have been made to feel.

But that isn't where our story is meant to end...

# Interwoven

As I have begun to delve deeper into and unpack my past, I realize it is just as pertinent, if not even more so, to dive into that of my parents as well. Not only have they heavily shaped my upbringing, but they also deserve the same chance for breakthrough, freedom and healing.

Anything buried and still affecting an individual will bleed out one way or another, either internally or externally. And if externally, by projection, passed usually unconsciously onto another.

Until the trauma and pain become unbearable. Until a person decides, I cannot live this way anymore. .. There must be another way. .. There has to be more than this. ..

# Mẹ (Mom)

My mom must have seen so much of herself in me. Not only appearance wise. We were both the second daughter in the family, had severe food allergies correlated with hives growing up, were a little more tomboy than princess. ..

I often wonder, well, quite a few things along with that. If she ever felt overshadowed by her older sister. If the traditions, values and challenges in her life made it difficult for her to feel and be all of herself, thus hindering her capacity to feel fully accepted and loved for who she was. And, in turn, making it harder for her to accept and love herself. If they instead made her bend for others to feel wanted, validated and approved...

She grew up most of her life without her biological father (who left to be with another woman) but became extremely close with her mom, spending most days with her, walking in different shops along the streets to pick up food or ingredients to make food from scratch for that day. There was no refrigerator she could recall. Her mom supported her in hobbies she had interest in, from cooking and baking to sewing. My mom would get to choose the fabrics she wanted and had fun creating clothes for her and her sister to wear.

She had two other siblings, an older and a younger brother. The three of them bonded over music. Her youngest brother played guitar well which influenced her and her older brother to become eager to learn. She ended up picking up chords so she could play by herself and sing along. Something she used to do a lot…

Sadly, both of her brothers passed due to different illnesses at separate times down the road. But music lived on in my mom. Even onstage years later, she played guitar and sang duets with a friend she met while in college to become a teacher. This friend also invited her to sing at church which she found to be very peaceful, beginning to have deep feelings of belief in God while singing worship songs.

I must have caught her passion for music and being with children :) She got to incorporate singing and guitar playing in her classes as a kindergarten teacher. It was saddening to hear she had to give up teaching when the Communists began taking over during the Viet

Nam War, affecting the way teachers had to
teach and the material they were given to teach.
In ways my mom could not agree with.

# Boat Escape/Inexplicable Faith

April 30th, 1975, was the fall of Saigon. The North took over South Viet Nam. Lots of families that worked for the South government or worked for the US Office in South Viet Nam had a chance to leave Saigon with US troops via big navy ships or airplanes in the Saigon airport. It was utter chaos. Overly crowded.

My mom decided to forego leaving as her best friend and her family chose to stay back at the last second. Her best friend's brother-in-law was still out fighting in the Navy in another part of Saigon.

Three years later, after the war ended, he, my mom's best friend and my mom began planning their escape by boat. The brother-in-law felt comfortable in his ability to navigate boats due to his Navy training and decided to buy one with a fisherman license.

That October, on a cold, windy night around midnight, my mom was given the chance to leave Saigon. It must have been a heartbreaking decision,  to leave her family and all that she knew behind, not knowing when, if ever, she would see them again…

Her best friend's brother-in-law did not ask for payment from her as she was like family to him. 50 others joined them on his small fishing boat. And off they went, moving as quietly as they could, holding their breath, hoping and praying that no Communist officer would catch them.

The water was fierce and unforgiving, especially at the point where the river met the ocean. Intense waves and strong winds continuously swept over, shaking their little boat until it was overcome with water.

Nervousness and fear began to grow all the more while cold and wetness seeped in. And then the engine died. The best friend's brother-in-law instructed everyone to throw heavy items, food, and clothes overboard to lighten the weight on the boat. They then began to haul as much water as they could out of the engine room with buckets so the brother-in-law could try to restart the engine.

The men and women on board, all they knew was to put their trust in God. Helping each other through prayer… It was an extremely emotional time for each person, seeming and feeling like this was a matter of life and death. Only God could help…

And then, miraculously, the engine started up again. They knew they had to go back to shore for safety. If the Communists caught them, they would for sure serve several months in prison.

.

.

My mom: "Thank You, God, for saving us on this trip."

.

.

In March 1979, they set out again from the same spot with almost the same 50 people. Together they left the shore in prayer... This time the riverbend was so calm and quiet. It was unbelievable in comparison to the first attempt…

They ended up making it safely to the Pulau Bidong Refugee Camp in Malaysia, where nearly 50,000 other refugees had come by boat. The Red Cross, churches, and other charities and organizations from different countries all around the world were there providing help, food, clothes and tents to live in. This Camp was where the paperwork of the refugees would be processed to sponsor them into a certain area in the US.

It was a hard and emotional goodbye for the 50 people on the boat my mom had been on, as each went their own way. But there they were, out of sheer, inexplicable Faith.

.

.


"For in Hope we were saved." (Romans 8:24)


...


My mom had no idea how long it would take for her to be sponsored, as the elderly, spouses, parents, and other immediate family members were priority. Then relatives. She had a family member in Chicago who she got in contact with, but, because he was her uncle, she knew she would have to wait (potentially up to four years!).

Every day, she would walk to the center of the island where paperwork was processed and names to be sponsored were announced, nearly bumping into others shoulder-to-shoulder because of how crowded it was. There was plenty of food to be seen and purchased, but my mom didn't even have a dime on her to spend.

Then one day, a woman walking in front of her turned to face her, asking whether she was my mom or my mom's sister. And my mom froze, heart tight and hardly beating, as it dawned on her that this was her dad's wife… It had been so long since they had last seen each other...

Má Ba (as my mom refers to her as) graciously agreed to add my mom onto her sponsorship papers to Kansas, where her sister lived, so my mom could bypass the need of approval for sponsorship in Chicago with her uncle.

My mom stayed one day in Kansas with Má Ba and her sister, then made her way to Chicago where she became homesick after a few months. It was winter then, her first experience with snow. The nights got so bright, it was hard for her to fall asleep…

She decided then that she wanted to move and find a job to support her mom and sister back in Viet Nam. It just so happened, her best friend from Viet Nam had now settled in California and, after getting back in touch, offered her a room to stay at in her house. So my mom jumped on a Greyhound bus. Once there, she felt at ease with the warmer weather and higher Asian population. She was fortunate to get a job in manufacturing that didn't require extensive skill nor much English.

Her coworker, who would become my sister's God Mother, one day asked if my mom wanted to meet a guy who seemed very nice and played tennis with her husband. So in 1985, this coworker held a potluck at her house for a viewing of the Superbowl. My mom walked into the living room with her favorite green coconut cake, and suddenly came face-to-face with my dad, who she recalls had a "familiar, friendly face," causing her to feel like she had already known him for a long time. It was God's planning she fully believes.

…

"Do not fear, for I am with you… I am your God. I will strengthen you… help you; I will uphold you." (Isaiah 41:10)

These words were printed on a small card hung on the fridge in the house I grew up in, and have stuck with me. They were the words my mom abided by. She says, "I refuse to be afraid, because God is with me."

And there is no doubt He has been.

# Bố (Dad)

My dad used to say, "Linnea Cookie from the cookie jar" to me when I was little, as a term of endearment I believe. I remember it making me feel special, seen and loved by him, because he did not use that with my older sister or my younger brother.

As we got older, the atmosphere changed. Not as much affection or one-on-one attention from him. Longer, later hours coming home from work. More frequent disputes with my mom and rage taken out on her. Some throwing of objects as well. My mom would often stay quiet, trying to protect us before becoming withdrawn from him. But I could tell she was hurting inside.

.

.

Let me take a moment to say, I feel there is a misconception about needing to keep what takes place at work separate from home. Your spouse is there to carry your burdens with you. And suppressed stress has to come out some way. If not processed internally gets released externally…

.

My dad's behavior and treatment also trickled
down to us kids. There were times after an
outrage that he would find my siblings and I,
who had sought out safety in our bedroom, to
tell us it was our fault.

I remember a moment when I was upset, sad and
crying, seeking solace in that room, that he came
to find me to tell me that crying doesn't help
anything and that I needed to be stronger.
Because he is my dad and I held reverence for
him, I decided he had a point. It didn't stop me
from crying though. I just did so more in private.

However, as I grew older, whenever he or
anyone with authority over me said something
that crossed or angered me, I felt so conflicted
inside, wanting to explode or scream at them,
but knowing I needed to remain respectful. I
don't think I had the words to express how I was
feeling then. It all just kind of boiled and lumped
in my throat.

Years later, while in college, my then-best friend
and I were out in downtown Seattle for fun. We
passed by a psychic reading place and decided
on a whim to go in. Upon scanning me, the
psychic stated my throat chakra was closed. It

did not register then, but I see the accuracy in it now.

...

I often wonder about my dad's upbringing and life before meeting my mom. There was plenty of care and love between parent and child, but not as much physical affection was shown. The love language seemed to be more through acts of service than anything else. My dad and his seven siblings supported themselves the best they could to take as much load and stress off their parents. He grew close with an older sister as well as with his younger brother and a younger sister, both of whom he helped take care of. Outside of home, he had a very social life, hanging out with friends at a coffee shop to get a drink and talk almost daily.

After high school, he was drafted into the Navy Academy to become a Navy officer. It sounded brutal. Day and night blurring. Doing anything and everything as commanded. Physically and mentally taxed. Not knowing when the next time he would get to shut his eyes or lay down and rest. But all so he and the others in training would be able to handle the same kind of strains that came up after completing the academy.

Before he got the chance to graduate, the Viet Nam War was ending and he and his family needed to immigrate to the US. However, not all of them could go at once. Only he and five of his siblings were able to fly out of Viet Nam to Camp Pendleton in San Diego, CA, as refugees. I imagine they were living in a constant state of survival, not having time to process any fears, sadness, grief, or other deep-seated emotions.

If it wasn't for the Navy officer pastor who picked them out of the sea of refugees, to sponsor and move them into his own home, who knows what would have become of them. But God had a plan. This was their chance at a new life with abundant possibilities. They took it upon themselves to learn English and find jobs to be able to afford an apartment of their own, not wanting to take advantage of their sponsor's generosity.

How courageous they had to be and how determined they were are nothing short of inspirational. Yet it is saddening as well, considering the circumstances.

My dad went on to graduate college with a software engineering degree, applying his strengths in math and sciences. Eventually he was introduced by an older tennis-playing friend to my mom. They had their first date, knew they wanted to be together immediately, and married six months later. Since both of their retirements in 2017, they have come to be more at peace with one another and with themselves.

# Anger/Rage

The Christian culture talks about self-control as it is a fruit of the Spirit (Galatians 5:22-23). However, it seems there is a fear around feeling anger. As though if you begin to feel angry, that means you are not exercising self-control. And that is just not true.

Anger is a valid emotion, as is every other emotion. Feeling anger rise up internally is a sign from your body telling you there has been a valued boundary within yourself (whether conscious or unconscious) that just got crossed in some way. The anger is a way of defending that value and protecting you from any potential danger or harm it senses.

There are ways to learn and become more aware of why a moment triggered that kind of feeling/reaction, as well as how to regulate your body and mind as the feeling of anger (or any other feeling or emotion typically labeled as "negative") arises.

Key: watch/take note of where in the body you start to get different sensations or feelings (e.g.

does your chest start to feel tight, heart beat faster, hands get clammy and begin to tense up? etc.), and then work with the most noticeable different sensation/feeling by being with it.

1. Acknowledge its existence - "Oh, I see you are there."

2. Send it what it is needing and wanting, usually to be fully seen.

For example, "That (statement/action/behavior) made you feel (whatever feelings you are feeling - belittled, unseen, unintelligent, etc.)? Yeah, I can see that. Tell me more. What else is coming up for you? Just know, you are brilliant and wonderfully made. God loves you. I love you."

3. Do something that brings you comfort and makes you feel loved.

For example, hug yourself or something you cherish (for my daughter, it would be a stuffed animal) in a nurturing way until you feel better; listen to your favorite tunes; eat or drink something comforting to your taste buds; go outside and be in nature; read something that breathes life, healing, encouragement, elation into you. Whatever the thing is that brings you

the most comfort and reinforces love for
yourself.

4. If 3 doesn't work, try something more
physical to move that pent up energy out.

Examples: moving and/or shaking out your
body, screaming all the feeling into a pillow,
releasing the feeling through physical activity
(hitting a punching bag, running, kickboxing,
etc.), doing some form of bodily flow and
breathwork (the Lion's Breath yogic pose or any
yoga, Tai Chi, etc.)

5. Once you feel in a more calm, regulated state,
if you feel comfortable talking to the person, let
them know how what they did or said made you
feel and how you would appreciate them treating
you, setting a boundary if necessary to prevent
further hurt feelings and mistreatment.

6. Realize a person's action and treatment is
never truly about you, but is a reflection of the
current state they are in - emotionally, physically
and/or mentally - along with any past and/or
external conditioning they may have. This is not
to excuse their treatment but to shed some light
on where they may have been coming from.

7. Release the weight of their words and actions.
You weren't meant to take and hang onto it.

8. Bid them healing as you do for yourself. Only
a person who is hurting would bleed out onto
another, unconsciously or not.


...


We need to normalize anything and everything
that makes us want to recede, that makes us
uncomfortable. Because that is how we grow in
humanity – meeting another where they are and
building each other up.

# Importance of Play in Adulthood

I feel like, as a society, from a young age, we are made to feel we have to work hard to earn. It is not a wrong message to ingrain. That money does not come freely and the amount of effort and quality put into work are important. After all, parent/s have to go to work to make money to affordfood, housing, transportation and everything else for the family. That is what we will have to do someday and be responsible for when we get older.

But then that takes away the whole concept of play, potentially as young as toddler/kindergarten years. We are made to believe that we need to strive for our living. To "grow up," "be mature" or "responsible" too soon.

Without play, the base for creativity and imagination is lost. The ability to find joy in the present moment can become harder to realize. Without these, living can feel rigid, mundane, repetitive. Essentially a to-do, get-done list set on futuristic happiness and success.

Even with God's presence in my life, I have found it difficult at times to feel and be thankful in challenging situations, especially continual ones, despite what 1 Thessalonians 5:18 states, to be thankful in all situations. But it was laid on my mind today to use play instead of making it like a chore. The energy in my body completely changed. It was more light. I noticed my mind was looking for different ways to approach the matter, versus already feeling bogged down, heavy in "this is happening again." I believe I tapped into the prefrontal cortex of my brain instead of the amygdala.

Why is play only associated with infants and the youngest of toddlers for exploring and learning? As adults, we talk about wishing we had the energy of young children. If we used play more, perhaps we could gather the desired level of energy and maybe even an ability to see situations differently - with less rigidity or repetitiveness. Less concern with the outcome. More freedom for openness, creativity and possibilities...

# Thank Yourself

Thank yourself. For all the tasks, no matter how small they might feel that you did that have gone unnoticed. For continuing to provide and give yourself sacrificially in all the ways that you did, whether for the ones you love or for those at work, in the community or elsewhere, while carrying the weight of heavy burdens on your mind and shoulders. For continuing to show up. Even get out of bed..

No one else may know just how hard it is. No one else may know how close you feel to losing it. To drowning. Suffocating. Giving up…

But there is strength in you. My Love. There is strength. There is Spirit in you. There is a Love that does not waver.

You see, you are gifting yourself into the world in some way, every day. Just by being here. Yes - you!

But don't forget to show up for yourself. You are worth being accepted, seen and embraced completely as you are. Not just by anyone, but by you especially!

You are amazing, brilliant, talented and unique. Worthy. Lovable. Loved.

So thank yourself when you've done something. Anything. Whether you've gone out of your way for someone or you've treated yourself to that (___) you've been eyeing for awhile… Others might not have noticed. But you don't have to wait for external expressions of gratitude.

You are a gift and offer so much into the world. Just by being you. Purely you :)

# The God I Know Does Not Ask You to Abandon Any Part of Yourself

It hurts my heart that there are those who feel they cannot be accepted, thus, ever loved, by God. That they would have to abandon any part of themselves to be. That is not right to me. God is for every individual on this earth.

I have family members and friends who are gay, lesbian, trans and queer, and let me tell you - they are some of the most authentic, caring, loving, fun, open, open-minded individuals with the biggest hearts I know. In their presence, I feel free to be completely myself. No hiding, no tweaking anything to fit in. Just an assured sense of belonging. That is pure acceptance and unconditional love.

That is reflective of the God I know, believe in and love. These family members and friends are a more accurate representation of all that God embodies than some who may call themselves devout Christians. Not to be blasphemous or anything.

But, consider this.

LGBTQ individuals have not chosen to abandon
themselves to be liked or accepted by others.
They have gathered enough wisdom and
courage, despite what society and some parts of
Christian culture might say, to choose
themselves. To love and accept themselves fully,
just as they have been created. By God.

To feel like you have to choose yourself or God -
that is never of God. He chooses you and will
always, relentlessly guide you in finding your
way back to choosing yourself.

# Being + Feeling Second to My Sister

My sister is very intelligent. Ambitious. She was
a straight-A student through grade school and
college (minus one A- which she was devastated
over). Throughout high school, she challenged
herself in multiple honors classes and was highly
involved in extracurriculars and leadership roles.
After graduating, because she had not felt
challenged enough in her first semester at
University of Washington, she applied to
Northwestern all the way in Chicago for the
program she wanted. Naturally, she was
accepted. Before even graduating there, she was
offered a well-paying job in consulting. It did
not come as a surprise as my sister has always
had a knack for connecting and being with
others in ways that made them want to befriend
her and/or have her as an ally. She has continued
to exercise that innate gift in her life, from
serving in a school district to becoming a yoga
teacher as of late.

Growing up, she had much poise and assurance
in herself. Long limbed, tall nosed, graceful.
There I was with a more pear-shaped figure,

thicker and shorter limbs, bushier, with a shorter, flatter and wider nose. Clumsier.

I did not think too much about looks then, and still do not, but I do remember being called "ugly" in elementary school, getting the comment "eww! Look at her legs!" from a random girl about my sister's age at the time while walking in Disneyland, and having someone who admired my sister completely dismiss me without even trying to get to know me in high school. Additionally, I got mediocre grades throughout grade school and did not attempt to push myself. My parents did not seem to care.

By that time I had believed and accepted I wouldn't ever become like my sister, but I was okay with that because I adored and looked up to her. She was good to me, supportive and always looking out, like older siblings do.

...

A part of me felt as though my mom favored her, the prized daughter, and our younger brother, the longed for son, over me. In the way she treated us. I felt as though I was the only one she got after for certain things as we got older. Like to be "faster" when I took my time walking or showering, but to also take better care of myself when I became apprehensive about taking showers or cleaning my ears, to name a few.

I grew up with severe eczema, dry skin issues, multiple food allergies, calcium deficiency, and earwax that would build up easily. To the extent that I would experience hearing loss when I tried to Q-tip it and have to go to the doctor to get it pumped out. My brother had asthma growing up as well as a severe peanut/nut allergy, but, to me, it never seemed like my mom made those out to be as much of a hardship as she did mine...

These things took longer for me to tend to. Sometimes I just didn't feel like I had enough energy to put into it, again. I just happened to be more problematic, complicated to take care of. And felt less loved by her because of that.

I have since confronted her about it, as scared as I was of how she would react. But she apologized and has backed away from that kind of treatment. I started feeling respected and accepted by her. Over time, our love for each other has blossomed, especially in recent years, as we have come to understand each other more.

# Hiding Talents to Be Seen as Humble

The one thing I was talented at growing up was tennis. That was our family activity/sport. My dad picked it up quickly a few years after immigrating to the US, having played ping pong during high school in Viet Nam. He enjoyed it so much, he played almost everyday and continues to do so :) He taught my siblings, mom and I how to play. It was some of the best times we had together, bonding and having fun. My brother has the most natural skill in it and has coached others since.

But let me rewind. Come my freshman year in high school, my sister, a senior that year, was on the varsity team, and I had made it onto junior varsity. One person in varsity got injured early in the season, and I was given the big opportunity to fill in. It was a joyous time, feeling like I was part of something bigger than myself and like I belonged and was valued.

We made it into district playoffs. Our school would announce daily over the intercom the news and updates about the team sports. My name started coming up. It did not take long for me to want to cringe away from the spotlight. To be quiet. To recede and be seen as humble, not boastful, even though I never once opened my mouth to share any kind of pride. All this by a classmate's unvoiced behavior towards me. Though I did not know her well, I had given value to her treatment towards me, not wanting to be disliked, and unconsciously choosing approval of others over my own.

From that moment, I chose to lose any identity found in that talent.

It ran into singing as well when I was older. Any time my siblings and I were together and a song came on that we all knew and liked, I would hesitate and refrain from joining in with their singing. I did not want to seem like I was competing or trying to show off. But it was highly self-restricting and robbed me of the joy I had always found from singing. Still, I refrained. Awhile later, my siblings became concerned and confronted me about it. I realized I had no valid reason to hold back. I now sing with them freely, anytime, anywhere.

But there is a difference between having pride and being arrogant in the talent and in oneself.

And then to use these talents as a way to glorify, give back to God, Who gifted these in us, is another thing.

Perhaps that is why singing has stuck with me but the tennis playing has since ebbed. I still play from time to time for fun and physical enjoyment, but it doesn't have the same pull on my heart as it used to, or as singing does.

# Stephen

My second year in high school, the first without my sister, was when the slut/whore labeling began. It altered my way of thinking greatly. I became solely tapped into the amygdala part of my brain. It scarred me for any close interaction, especially with members of the opposite gender, in the years following. So much so that I would become selectively mute. Single males. Males with partners already. I did not want to seem like I was flirting, trying to steal anyone. They did not have much interest in me anyway... The rare ones who did, did not want me in the way I hoped...

Then Stephen came along. When I was not trying for anything. And he altered all of that. ..

We almost missed each other. This was three years after finishing college. He grew up in Maryland but was out for a yearlong stint with Idaho Fish and Game in Salmon. I was offered two community service AmeriCorps positions, also yearlong, about the same time. One in Annapolis, Maryland (roughly 43 miles away from where he grew up), the other also in Salmon.

It was a difficult decision for me. Both offered exciting, from-the-ground-up opportunities as well as new experiences. I had never been to either state. After a thorough pro-con list for each and much consideration, I nearly went with Annapolis but decided on Salmon.

I had a hard time adjusting once out there. This was the furthest and longest time away I had been from home or anyone I knew. To a very small rural town, in the middle of nowhere, three hours away from the nearest airport.

But the mountains there - the mountains were gorgeous. Peaceful. Calming. Alive. We were at the base of the Beaverheads. I would often go on strolls to see them closer, and on the way pass by horses, pigs, chickens, sheep - animals of all kinds - up close, just on the other side of the wooden logged fence.

When winter came, it looked like Heaven was coming down on those mountains, dusting the earth. Though it was probably the coldest winter I have experienced, it was the most beautiful.

Most pristine. My heart began to grow fond of this town.

Spring rolled along. My coworkers and I were deeply involved with the community by that time. Meaningful work to address food insecurity and hunger with local food systems - growing food from seed in a community garden; joining in with the Sacajawea Center to provide gardening classes for youth; holding simple-to-make-and-healthy-recipe cooking classes in the schools and for the public; partnering with local farmers, educators, creators and interested individuals to put on agricultural workshops along with other community events.

That is when I first got to interact with him – Stephen. He showed up at one of the cooking classes we offered and helped with a dill yogurt dip I was also contributing to :) He came to a few other classes but we did not interact much more… I saw him once or twice after that around town, but nothing became of it.

Then it was summer. The annual White Water Festival to kickoff the season. Kayak relay races, live music, food galore. I spotted him across this one small bridge. He was drinking something, a can in one hand. But he was not making eye contact, so I went on my way.

A bit later, I was sitting down with my coworkers and a few of their friends as the live music began to play. Abruptly, he appeared and just sat down right next to me, striking up a conversation. It felt so comfortable and easy to talk to and be with him, as if I had already known him.

We spent the rest of the evening talking and being in each other's company. Even having our first "dance" – hand-in-hand in front of the stage where the live music was, spinning in circles, not knowing the other was also as dizzy and close to throwing up… Not wanting to ruin the moment.

I had a few other firsts with him. My first time floating in a raft on the water where I ended up falling out. Lol:) It was still fun though. What a way to view the scenery! Also being surprised with several small, beautiful handpicked bouquets of hydrangeas along with three cartons of ice cream (each with peanut butter, his favorite, but which I am allergic to, though he had no way of knowing) on my birthday. It was such a sweet gesture. Although he continued to

apologize when he found out, little did he know
he had already begun to build a permanent place
in my heart.

We went to Williams Lake, not too far out of
town, shortly after and hiked in until we reached
the lake. He did these magnificently magical and
accurate bird call sounds with his voice (which I
would later discover he learned in college) that
actually drew birds to him. I was so taken in! It
felt as though we were the only ones there...

Out of nowhere, I heard a booming voice say to
me, "You are going to learn to love this man."
And I knew it was God's. And I knew He was
right. How I have come to love Stephen... and
how he has loved me - beyond all expectation
and measure - and has helped me in learning to
see myself as someone worth loving. ♡

...

God intended us to meet in the most unlikely of
places, out of the most unlikely of
circumstances, just as He did my parents.

"All things work together for good for those who
love God." (Romans 8:28)

# Intrusive Thoughts As A Gift

As I have come into more of my own, who I am in God, away from others' perceptions and expectations of me, I have found more strength, certainty and courage in my voice - my opinions, thoughts, values, beliefs and faith. But I have also noticed certain intrusive thoughts come up more strongly when I use my voice. "Just be quiet" in particular. Trying to silence me. Trying to make me feel shame, belittled, doubtful of myself.

These are all feelings and thoughts of the past. Of which I no longer need to hold onto. Of which I do not because my identity in God is my truth. That is what I hold onto now.

I am grateful to these intrusive thoughts, for without having experienced them firsthand so belligerently, I might still be deep in the grips of all the things I internalized and came to believe of myself that were not true. That kept me from fully knowing and feeling the Infinite Love of God and the power of His Healing Grace.

These thoughts have become a gift in disguise.

# How I Want to Live – For God. Like Jesus.

It is rather sad to me that there are those who say, to those who believe in God, He is the one inventing the troubles in the world. That He is putting them here. Whether to punish and/or harm – that is unclear what they believe.

But that is so far from the truth.

As human beings, we have been given the privilege of freewill. It ranges between acting out of the most altruistic of intentions or from a place of deep hurt, pain, sadness, anger and/or resentment.

But this also is influenced out of our own consciousness, mindfulness of ourselves. Whether there are still things we continue to hang onto and grapple with letting go of or forgiving. Whether we have discovered a capacity to hold and openly send compassion to ourselves and all others when adversity, struggles, mistakes come up. Recognizing we are more like one another than we are different. Recognizing we are all faulty somewhere, at some point, and are in need of love, grace and connection.

This is God. He knows each one of us. He created us. He cares for you and me. He does not want to punish or harm us. But in giving freewill, He cannot prevent things from occurring organically out of collective human actions.

He vows to protect those who believe in Him. He vows to make good out of despair and darkness. He is a giver of Hope and Light. He freely pours out Grace.

Though I cannot explain unexpected sickness, deaths or other unwanted occurrences, I have found, through my own experiences, that if we desire to be/live/walk like Jesus - if loving God as ourselves + others and surrendering our lives to Him are the focus of our heart - we will be made to lose all the outer material, layers that we picked up along the way that no longer serve a purpose.

Jesus was a carpenter (Mark 6:3), a servant. Humble. Living very low key, out of the spotlight. He acted each moment of his earthly life out of the loving, kind, patient, compassionate guidance of the Holy Spirit. The internal compass we have access to from God while on earth.

This is how I want to live – For God. Like Jesus.

# Come As You Are



Trying to capture what we are as a human being. There is so much inside each of us, just dying to be let out. To be shared. All that we have been through, coupled with our interests and beliefs, to become who we are. There is a lot of pain, heartache, struggle we go through and endure, but also joy, life, love, laughter...

To come as we are in my mind means being vulnerable, showing up with everything we are - mistakes, fears, doubts, ups, downs, everything in between - and being welcoming and embracing of it all as well as holding grace for every other being to show up the same way, in any and all forms.

That is how God seeks us to be in our relationship with Him. Intimately. Openly. Honestly. A healthily growing bond full of compassion and trust if we let it.

We do not have to be anything aside from who we are and what we feel at any given moment to commune with God. To feel we can call out to Him. To belong anywhere. To feel and be seen and heard, unjudged.

"Just come as you are and I will sit with you. No matter what it is. No matter who you are, your status, where you came from, your past or present. I will sit with you and I will be with you. Through this. And anything you want Me to be a part of thereafter. This isn't too much for Me. It won't scare Me away. You do not have to change anything, improve, be any better in order for Me to be here with you."

~ Just come as you are. ~

# How Living Out Faith is Akin to Being Vulnerable

Faith and the decision to follow God/be a disciple of Jesus, willingly, is akin to being vulnerable in that you are putting all your belief out there, in the forefront, on the line. No hiding or blanketing, softening anything.

There may be controversy, scorn, rejection, even hate out of it. There will be persecution. Possible death. But that is okay. Because you are with the One who has already given you a way through. Victory over it. Through Jesus Christ. No matter what, you are with Him and He is with you, whether on earth or in Heaven. You can stand firm in these knowings, in these truths. A mountain, though maybe shaken, unmoved.

The suffering on earth, no matter how difficult and long it lasts, can be viewed as a privilege that God trusts you as a disciple of Jesus to endure it all in submission, surrender to His will and timing, having faith, belief, trust that the goodness of Him and His works will be glorified through it.

That is how I am choosing to see suffering from now on. A privilege. An offering. A way to bring others close/closer to God. A way that brings me closer to Him.

# Unlocking and Losing
# "Sorry"

"Sorry" I would say when I was made to feel I was in the way.

"Sorry" I would say when I was made to feel I was taking too much time.

"Sorry" I would say when I began stumbling over the words coming out of my mouth.

"Sorry" if I said something that wasn't agreed with.

"Sorry" after asking for something I needed, even help. Especially help.

"Sorry" after being told I didn't need to be sorry…
.

.


These all came from a place where I felt I was at fault and to blame for other people's treatment and behavior towards me.

But as I have grown in my relationship with God, I have come to discover an identity in Him that is complete and unshakable.

Though I have my quirks and make mistakes, I know and fully believe God loves me and still deems me worthy, even with those things.

We are not meant to be perfect. Otherwise there would be no need for Him to have sent His only Son down as a sacrifice for our sins and a gateway for our atonement.

The way He looks at me and loves me - unconditionally, embracing all of me while guiding me without reprimand - is what has led me to rediscovering my own worth and belief, to have more grace and compassion for myself and others, as well as accepting and loving all of what makes me me.

To me, worth is recognizing respect in and for oneself, and then recognizing that equally in others.

For too long I had been made to be what I thought was "humble," "respectful" and "nice" - not standing up for myself, not voicing anything that could bring any kind of conflict, keeping outer peace, pleasing others so they wouldn't feel uncomfortable. And while "turning the other cheek" is called for and can be encouraged in a fair amount of situations, especially when we find we are close to judging prematurely or at all, it should not be at the cost of our inner peace. Our own needs. Our own voice. Our own belief and worth in ourselves.

.

.

Proverbs 28:1 says, "The wicked flee when no one is pursuing, but the righteous are bold as a lion."

.

.

We are meant to be bold in what is righteous in God's eyes, in our treatment towards others as well as ourselves; and in our faith, not timid in the way we carry or voice it. Bold in our identity we hold in God. Bold in our testimony.

We are God's. Each a child of God. Who deemed us worthy to be adopted, saved, healed and loved like no other by Him.

He gave everything to you. To me. To each one of us. So we could have Life. So we could know, feel, increase in and offer: Perfect Love. Joy. Grace. Mercy. Communion. Healing.

Why wouldn't I give myself completely for
Him? My 100%. Surrendered. Laying it all on
the line. No matter the cost.

.

.


"It is no longer I who live but Christ Jesus who
lives in me. The life I now live in the body, I live
by faith in the Son of God, who loved me and
gave Himself for me." (Galatians 2:20-21)

# Mayli as My Mom, Spirit Unhindered

When I look at and watch my daughter, I see so much of my mom in her. The tenacious spirit, unhindered; vivacity for life; big, giving, caring, tender heart.

I pray God covers her every day, and guides and molds her into who she is meant to be. Into who she has already been created to be. Child of Light (Ephesians 5:8). Faith and Spirit of a Lion.

Don't let the world make you feel you have to compromise any part of yourself to be accepted. To be worthy. You already belong in the eyes and heart of The Most High.

.

.


"Thus says the Lord, who created you, Jacob, and formed you, Israel: Do not fear, for I have redeemed you; I have called you by name: you are Mine." (Isaiah 43:1)

# Emmanuel

~ Emmanuel ~ God with us.


"The light shines in the darkness, and the darkness did not overcome it." (John 1:5)


...


Hope –
Intangible yet ever so existent
Abstractly within reach

My eyes look up to the sky, searching
Searching for a way out
A way through
For more strength out of struggle
For more relief out of this pain
For more healing from suffering and this seeming defeat
For more comfort and trust in this chaos
For more acceptance, compassion, and love out of this division and hatred.
These wars.
These indignities.

How can we be one - United, Together; Body of
Christ - if we cannot even be with our own
selves peacefully. ..

But not of our own doing.
Only He could do the unthinkable
Unravel, patiently, by your side.

The Light of the World
Prince of Peace
Protector
Redeemer
Faithful
Healer
Grace
Forgiving
Merciful
Love

Perfect, Unconditional, Infinite

Eternal.

No matter the wavering circumstances, God is
unchanging, and so, too, is our beacon of Hope.

9 789363 319882